Reclaiming Calla Lilies

Sarah Elizabeth Moreman

Reclaiming Calla Lilies © 2023 Sarah Elizabeth Moreman

All rights reserved.

No part of this publication may be reproduced, stored in a retrieval system, or transmitted, in any form or by any means, electronic, mechanical, photocopying, recording or otherwise, without the prior written permission of the presenters.

Sarah Elizabeth Moreman asserts the moral right to be identified as author of this work.

Presentation by *BookLeaf Publishing*

Web: www.bookleafpub.com

E-mail: info@bookleafpub.com

ISBN: 9789357212663

First edition 2023

Choosing what to say and share is not without careful consideration to the Almighty One Who has my heart in His loving hands.

To the ones who may feel encouragement from reading these poems.

ACKNOWLEDGEMENT

The calla lilies as a promise of resilience -- I acknowledge that without what I had been through, I would not be where I am today. I give thanks to the two who have led me to this point in life, writing poetry with them in mind to better understand the what ifs and the whys. These two did encourage me to write, and here I am writing.

PREFACE

While purity, innocence, and beauty are commonly associated with this elegant flower, these poems focus more on the deeper meaning of rebirth, resurrection, resilience. Through her own words, may they be raw and not necessarily organized, the writer shares her thinking process with calla lilies as the emblematic scar of joy and peace.

returning to calla lilies

Calla lilies chosen with hope,
yet crushed into broken colored crystal that
swept away,
one sliver of leaf-petal at a time
whenever the clandestine phone lit up, ringing.

walked away, my ponytail swinging across my
back,
feeling the dark eyes piercing through my
shoulder blades,
yet the roped knot in my stomach loosened
each step away from the crushed calla lilies,

…once white, now crushed and carelessly
breathed away.

refused to have to do anything with the
leaf-petaled flower,
even though their classy beauty appreciated.
The juxtaposition of hope and despair.
The ambivalence.

not until having walked past,
this metal piece snagged my consciousness
ironically after having had endured yet another

crushing—must have forgiven truly and with peace.

these malleable iron pieces
welded and shaped like calla lilies.
bending one around a thumb,
admiring this one calla lily of metal.

the accent plates of the past
replaced with iron,
with forgiveness,
with peace.

Elegant moment of silent connection

Long nights of poring over page layouts,
alert for any discrepancies or errors,
wanting aesthetically pleasing perfection
in carrying out the purpose of our timed
keepsake.

Like the field of calla lilies bursting with color,
the annuals burst forth and spread out among
many
to take home and flip over each page
of year-long memories captured.

…reverence captured in such a thriving
environment.

The sun was shining bright, placing the
belonged one
on the shelf only to be taken out whenever the
need
to remember arises.
It was time to look up.

Looking up was what I did.
After a few weeks already at the lab,

having changed out of the navy overalls and
black boots
and back into my shirt and shorts.

The sun was shining bright when I looked up
after laughing with my friends as we walked
across
the field. As I looked up, the sun seemed to
pause.
The breeze, the sounds, the traffic—all paused.

I felt this sense of expectation as if I should
remember and
revere this moment—I looked, and he waved.
I felt that reverence, that expectation, that
connection
in this elegant moment of silence.

Trio Plum

The desire to express persisted
as I huddled with other girl scouts,
brainstorming a utopia,
our own little society.

Trio Plum, I declared.
The velvety coloring of the
deep purple, steeping deeper into
midnight blackness.

…the royalty in such a worldview.

The trailing of silver ribbons
in the breeze as we sang our anthem.
Trio Plum was the ideal embodying
what I believed about humanity.

What I would do to make
Trio Plum a reality.
Nevertheless, the opposite happened…
It was hell.

It was hell that stealthily took away
my deep-held understanding and
perception of what the world should be.
Culture shock at its finest.

Yet the calla lily has richness in the color of a plum,
where the royalty of hope and conviction reigns,
bringing forth the solid bloom of faith.
Strength in its tubular form.

It is the deepest part of the purpleness,
The midnight blackness, that quieted my soul
as I sought His face. He was and still is the
Trio Plum I had been searching for and now
found.

Four

Four was such a deadly number, meaning death.
Yet it fits as I turned around after having walked away,
To watch helplessly the train hurtling faster and faster
To its destructive wrecking end.

When the ink was barely dry on paper,
I drove the Darth Vader across fields under the great big sky,
Wearing a Stetson, with a bittersweet wonder at life.
She and I refused to accept any room with the number four.

…four epitomizes destruction, death, not stability.

Must avoid the number four at all costs—or go back and
start over yet with damning knowledge.
The calla lily, once pure in its whiteness, is now dirty
and shredded, void of any hope for rejuvenation.

I had tried, tried, tried, tried
To forgive each day, to forget the past moments
Yet my prayers were not answered
At least not in the way I wanted.

Forgiveness was hard for me to feel in my heart
As I began each day the fourth hour after waking up.
It was the fourth week when I realized I was fooled.
It was the fourth month when I realized I was deceived.

It was the fourth year when I realized faith was the only way.
After the fourth try of seeking hope in flesh, I chose to lay
My anguish cares at His feet by falling onto my face
To pray.

For years, the fourth hour after walking up each day
was when I cried out onto the ruled paper,
seeing the letters sloppily curved into words as I desperately
asked to forgive not four times, but seventy times seven.

Five

They crowned her with such an unsavory name,
which signified her head position among many others.
I did not think of such unsavory name, but
I could not bring myself to utter her real name.

Her real name rhymes with mine.
Two sets of four years, she stole what was promised
to me to have and to hold for better, for worse.
Destroying her own and mine what should be cherished.

…the meaning of five held a sharp coldness of betrayal.

After the darkness fell each night,
After the food was picked at and pushed aside,
After the dishes were washed and put away,
I hurried upstairs to shut out the cruelty of isolation.

Isolation from repeated rejection of my willingness…

Isolation from repeated denunciation of my being too much…
Isolation from repeated condemnation of my requests…
Isolation from repeated ignorance of my being.

Choosing to savor in these moments takes strength
as I desperately sought freedom in Him.
These savory moments gradually strengthened me
as I chose to seek beyond what I saw with my own eyes.

The Word seeped into the marrow of my bones
as I hungrily devoured for answers.
No longer did I feel despair and loneliness, because
I found hope.

Blueness painting the rites of passage

Six years. It took six years to get here
And yet only for a time
when we seemed to be in touch with
each other—as a nod to the blue calla lilies.

The smoke, the feel, the touch
all were blue in varying hues
as the butterflies slowly flutter in hope
as I looked into his eyes.

…what does the blue signify with us?

The rushing of waters…
The roaring of War Eagles…
The rippling of wishes…
The ruining of hopes

as I looked into her eyes,
past her eyes, into her own soul.
The young one wanted the same hopes that I was promised,
for she believed in them.

Yet another six years passed

before she reached out with courage
and wisdom-earned determination for
redemption.
I chose the unlikely

as I looked into her eyes,
past her eyes, into her own soul.
Our shared understanding blazed,
the blue fires forging redemptive healing.

planting my choices, watering with my tears

What He wants is a relationship, not babblings and anxieties.
What He wants us to grasp is real, not fake.
We are to hold on to what is precious, not cast them before swine.
We are to hold on to trusting in Him, not fall sideways for quicker results.

If only we trust in Him that good things will come in His time, not ours.
If only Eve holds on to the one command rather than fall sideways, yet that tree
of redemption is already planted. In the shadows of this Edenic tree where Eve's tears had soaked into darkness, blossomed white calla lilies that shone with a pearly sheen.

…He loves and forgives already before we ask Him.

Even though I pulled my arm away after having heard the words,
"You deserve to be treasured like a princess."
Even though I pulled away after being told,

"I am not giving my blessing."

I still crawled back to the roots of that tree of redemption,
to shed my own tears of failure, of having sinned,
knowing that the tears of mine were being used,
the results in the form of calla lilies blossoming.

I watched Him plant all my seeds, both good and bad, into the soil.
He then brought out this bottle that held my tears from over a decade and half, letting
a few drops spill out onto the dirt, where my seeds were deeply buried.
He set the bottle down and then pulled me into His embrace.

He whispered to my soul, telling me to be patient.
The calla lilies would return,
In His time, not my time.
In His arms, I fell into restful waiting.

Sharp boldness of red

Red flags. Why could we not heed them?
Why could we not listen to others' loving warnings to help us
avoid making the same mistakes as they made?
Red flags, the sharp boldness of color in these red flags.

Was it pride? Was it the insistence that the outcome would be different
because we believed we were that special?
We wanted to be revered as that special that those who made such promises
actually kept them.

…the sharp boldness of red should not be dismissed.

No matter what we desperately wanted to believe or hope,
The sharp boldness of red would not diminish or dim.
No matter how much we desired or even thought we needed,
We must not dismiss the glaring sirens of red.

He gave us the feelings of intuition, and we must listen.
We must not quiet the disquiet when we are feeling conviction.
He gave us the feelings of intuition to protect us,
To prepare us, to strengthen us, to be used for His master plan.

I chose to embrace the sharp boldness of red as a symbol of His love,
The sharp boldness of red coursing through His veins, forgiving me
for having rebelled against His love, redeeming me of my transgressions,
clearing away the veil that separated us.

I embraced the sharp boldness of red by bringing in reminders
In the form of bloodred calla lilies.
Courage and determination replacing fear and anxiety,
Doing away with bitterness—thus, inviting resurrection of hope.

Bottom of the ninth

I was confused. I ruminated.
I did not understand. I waited.
Yet I waited for him to initiate,
because he was the man, not me.

Not knowing where I stood, I waited.
I respected his wishes when he told me
to not talk to certain persons.
Therefore, I did not talk to these certain persons.

…that final and critical moment of a such saga.

How could I not say hi or Merry Christmas though?
After all the times I respected his wishes, I received backlash.
Shush, he narrowed his eyes, finger at his lips.
Blood seemed to be drained
completely out of me, leaving me out of breath.

Keeping myself together, I whispered,
    "May I have your permission to go for a walk?"
The look on his face clanged that final nail,
Crushing the pink calla lilies of appreciation.

The crushed bits of the pink leaf petals scattered
in the dark starry night,
among the pristine whiteness of snow as I let out
shuddery breaths
while focusing to keep together my shushed
form,
unwilling to add to the wetness of the sidewalks
ensconced by evergreens.

Upon my return, the devastation that I could not
remember
due to the effects of being shushed panned out to
months and months
of heart-rending tension with unresolved needs
only to end
with treacherous abandon.

The writer's ambivalence

"Any writer would love to live here and write,"
he said.
Hearing him speak those words sounded
accusing.
In that moment, I felt fear.
In that moment, I felt I was losing him.

Why did he not love me?
He chose me, and yet he seemed tiring of me
only weeks
after we promised forever to each other.
Staring out at the backdrop of tree-covered
mountains and the river,

…how could I write? How could I not write?

The pen, carefully chosen, was poised over the
paper
as I took in the long scratchy wisps of the
pampas grass hugging
the crossties that bordered the backyard. The
river quieted down
into a soothing ripple from the pandemonium of
the day.

The lowering sun beckoned me to write. Letting out a sigh, I lowered
the pen, not knowing what to write, yet forcing myself.
I watched the words form on paper as I refused to let myself
think.

I could not let myself think while he was home; otherwise, he
would know what was going on through my mind.
He often told me, "Do not think."
He knew me too well.

He knew what to say at the right time to spur me into doing something he wanted me to do.
And…subsequently,
I became afraid to write when he was around and
also even when he was not around.

Thanksgiving of uncertainty

Uncertainty stole away peace as the dressing finished baking while I bacon-fried the ham,
Trying to keep the cornbread, sweet potato casserole, and green beans warm,
The dining table set with fine china and silver on top of red jacquard tablecloth,
Tossing out melting ice cubes and replacing in the crystal with the fresh.

Uncertainty turned anticipation to bewilderment As the clock mocked me.
No text messages, and I could not talk on the phone.
Oh, how I wish I could.

…such frustration with being hearing impaired.

If I could talk on the phone, I would feel better hearing his voice.
If I could talk on the phone, I would feel better knowing he was okay.
IF I could hear him on the phone, would he appreciate my being concerned?
IF I could hear him on the phone, would he love me more?

The food cold and hard as I tried to smile when he came in.
Silence as he grabbed a plate not from the dining table, but from the cabinet.
I followed his lead, and we sat in the living room.
The television on, blaring out.

Then abruptly muted after a quiet question was asked.
Reactionary responses given that left more questions in the air, unwilling to be asked.
Plates still loaded with barely eaten food carried back to the kitchen,
One heart stumbling in even deeper uncertainty.

Fumbling a Styrofoam cup, filling it up with the precise amount of ice before
pouring in the Dr. Pepper, carefully carrying it to him.
At his dismissive nod, I returned to the kitchen to finish
scraping off food from the dishes.

Making the demons flee

Pushing deep down the bulbs that should transform into
midnight violet beauties of calla lilies, feeling the dirt
with my fingers brought out a sense of rightness.
I was not going to get some calla lilies, but I am glad I did.

I was not going to have to do anything with this leaf petaled flower
for the memories it flares up in my brain.
However, time has passed, along with my perception having
returned to its state of clarity, purpose, and faith.

…reclaiming calla lilies for myself, making the demons flee.

Making the demons flee by having confidence in Him.
Only He can be my portion, no other human being
could ever fulfill me, could ever make me happy.
Even though I cannot hear in the way others do, I have Him.

Planting those midnight violet calla lilies,
Being patient with the growth through failures and triumphs,
Learning by leaning on Him and not by my own understanding,
my foundation is established on the Rock.

No other human being is infallible.
Therefore, I should fear no man.
Only in Him shall I fear with trust, knowing He has me
under His wings.

Any failures and fiery trials I endure help remind me of my own
humanness, that I can only do all things through Him who strengthens me.
As long as I humble myself under His mighty hand, He will uplift me,
making the demons flee.

green with letting go

Longing for that white picket fence
while waiting for him to finally see
the efforts I have been making
to make that longing no longer a dream

Yet, yet I have been told to wait.
I felt led to believe that my longings
to welcome many to our home
were not welcomed.

…yet, yet I saw how others have houses full.

Rather than being still in my waiting,
weeding the flowerbeds
planting bulbs, planting dreams
with hopes to bloom with expectation.

The grass is green here, not over there,
because the growth comes from my own hands.
The grass is green here, not over there.
Letting go may be the only way to grow

Letting go may seem counterintuitive
when, not if, I stop watering with my tears.
The rivulets dotting the leaf petals that bloomed

slowly, then quickly, trickle down to the green grass.

Seeing the water in the grass reflecting the blue skies,
the depths of my tears reaching far down
into the dark damp soil, letting go is the only way
to prevent root rot of the soul.

Another Thanksgiving of despair

Why was I feeling this sense of impending doom?
Watching and waiting for him to show me love
By giving me what I asked—quality time.
His idea of quality time differed from mine.

James Bond simply because…
not really for me…even shooed away the young,
gave more time to his cats than me, yet
not really for me…but for himself.

…when would I ever matter?

Despair slowly smothering me as I waited for him to acknowledge
how important I was to him, that I mattered to him. Instead,
he ended the evening with confessions. The confessions he did not realize
that I picked up through his storytelling, which only increased my despair.

Tears were hard to hide as my heart slowly cracked

as more confessions came. I refused to see what he was telling me,
especially when it came to the stainless steel—which turned
the promise of a future into abandonment.

The stainless steel mattered more.
Then, the turkey was over fried.
The snow was not blinding as I drove back—yet only brought
me out of the foggy delusions of grandeur.

Yet I still refused to let go, and He had to let me go,
knowing that I would be crushed, grinded, and abandoned.
Yet He is still weaving me into His Story
that someday I would understand.

fiery orange sunsets

The roars fill the jungle as the sun is setting,
streaking across the sky
with orange sunsets, glorifying the One Who
keeps me steady.
Touching the lone calla lily burns as its tiny
needles
prick painful memories back to mind.

Admiring the lone calla lily from afar, its burnt
color
that reminds me of the orange sunsets, such
radiant glory
sustains me as I prodigiously return home.
Never forgetting the burning pain, yet…

…the burning of such orange fierceness purifies.

No matter how many orange sunsets
that flame with such opalescent fierceness,
His presence fills me with fiery purpose
and willingness to be still.

He fights for me as I stand still.
Being silent calls for strength and contentment,
knowing that He sees the future,
knowing that His ways are higher than mine.

Being silent calls for fierce determination,
as I hope in my fierce Warrior,
as the eagle soars into the azure,
as the tiger roars into deafening silence.

The roars fill the jungle
as the fiery orange sunsets glow
with the glory of the One who bestows
such fierceness in having the sense of rightness
to be still.

mauve softness

Why did I fear man? Why did I let myself give in to fear?
I used to be strong, unbendable in my resolve
to be perfect, the solidness of purple.
I yearned for my perfection to be revered.

Even with such perfection, it was not treasured.
Instead, mud splattered over my pristineness.
The mud of their uncertainty, deceit, hatred, and pride smeared,
darkening the leaf petals of my heart.

…such darkness held back the true love of serving others.

Unwilling to drown in the tears of anguish and unrequited,
I sought the sunlight of His grace.
The more I sought His face, the more radiance
brightened my damned, mocked perfection.

No longer stiff and unyielding,
my perfection softened into mauve.
With His gentle caring fingers, He wiped away
the muddiness with His own tears.

I could feel His heart ache as
He breathed dry the soppy wetness of the soil,
firming the foundation of His love and grace,
His radiance softening my resolve.

No longer darkened with dismissiveness
and cruelty, I slowly reached back to
what I once knew about love and grace,
which is to esteem others above the self.

meaning of sacrifice

Do not be a martyr, she said.
Leave now, do not cleave with him.
Yet I rebelled, wanting my love to be real,
not having to go through the heartbreak.

Do not be a martyr, she said.
She tried to get me to see the stars
illuminating brilliantly out of the window
as she shared her own breaking heart.

…yet I rebelled, wanting my love to be real.

Promises veiled with hidden revenge,
pearls gifted with intent to startle,
diamonds given with secretive cruelty,
purity taken on the eve of losing respect.

The knot tightened as to choke out any remaining
stubbornness to prove that my love was real.
What was love?
What is love?

Being a martyr does not mean to deny faith.
Being a martyr means to deny the self, of pride.

I thought what I did was worthy as a sacrifice,
as to love beyond my own expectations.

I thought by denying myself would draw him
closer to Him, that martyring myself would be
worth it.
Time told me that my sacrifice should be
for Him, not to save him.

hearing the honey

knot in the stomach twisting tighter
bands around the cerebrum sharpened like
barbed wire
breathing controlled as to not be admonished
hearing the honey in his voice

fear muted me as i listened to that honey in his
voice
vastly juxtaposing from the one directed at me
only minutes earlier, which shoved me into
stunned
bewilderment, resulting in questioning myself

…the honey in his voice prickled the imminent
ominous

raging why as i ran upstairs, to get away
from having to hear the honey in his voice
ever since that first night of awareness
i hear the honey in his voice more each night

why could i not receive such regard
barbed wire around the cerebrum tightening
cerebellum hot with paralyzed indecisiveness
breathing controlled as to not be ridiculed

night and day started to merge into pleading in prayer
knees burned, eyes scratchy, fingers stronger from writing
heart still resolute to forgive, yet emotions did not feel forgiving
lips stretched when prompted by others

too much honey opened my listening heart to the Word,
wisdom filled with knowledge and truth, thus bringing forth
the words sweeter than honey, bringing balm to my soul,
metabolizing the honey in his voice into purpose woven into His story

welded vessel

Sliding the necklace with the metal three calla lilies
around my neck, the matching bracelet, earrings, and ring
already in place. The precise click-clack of my heels
as I leave my place.

An hour later, standing before those younger,
their pens moving across college-ruled sheets of paper
"Stop. Please move the papers up front."
The precise click-clack of my heels as I collect the papers.

…welded stronger, purpose stronger.

Touching the metal resting at the base of my neck,
I feel the intricate design of the calla lilies before speaking.
"Writing is more than simply writing.
It gives us a powerful way to express our voices."

I smile at the younger whose listening faces
remind me the why and how I am standing right
here
I am a vessel, a voice, for others to listen
not to the actual me—more, to Him.

The unwillingness to respect the reality of
danger, the devastation
in the wake of my foolishness, the savagery in
my journey,
shattering the illusions both in the mind and
body.
I crawled back rest at His feet, seeking His face.

I am only a vessel, a vase shattered and put back
together.
I am only a vessel, a welded vase forged with
stronger metal
of calla lilies to hold the much softer,
more real leaf petals of Truth and Living Water.

growing enlightened

vague understanding, blissfully ignorant,
spiritually unawakened, stubbornly insistent,
an abstract painting rather than concrete sculpture
of the garden no longer thanks to the first taste of sin.

the wise, the elders, listen to them,
no matter advanced the mechanization,
nothing can or should replace the experience and wisdom
tis the order of things.

…wisdom can only be gained through growth.

although sturdy and can grow anywhere, the calla lily
blooms after three leaves countenanced,
fragrance delicate and subtle that one must lean closer
as one must lean closer to Him

stubbornness blinded, instilling that insistence
for a stronger scent, whereas He patiently waits

like a gentleman with a lady, the depth of her emotions
plunging further the more faux fulfillment in the self

let the soft leaf petals rise past many blades
open to the glory of wisdom, blushing into mauve,
exemplifying robustness in the order of things
through maturation

the calla lily no longer an abstract painting
now a concrete sculpture tangible, albeit supple
now awakened spiritually, pliant to see
seeing and listening, growing towards the Light

the lone calla lily

elegance is in the simplicity.
one is enough, no need to stray,
commitment is more than a feeling,
for the last page, one is to stay.

His voice trailing off even on the last period,
yet two more dots intentionally…eternal gift of staying
through the willingness to trust,
even as a lone calla lily

…the elegance of a lone calla lily

blessing the lone calla lily
with distinct homage, to share
the beauty in its simplicity, its form
remarkable to draw others to the Creator

fearfully and wonderfully notable
to signify what truly matters,
the grand love story of all time
comes from redemption.

redemption is reunion
the lone calla lily is never alone

even when others have been gathered
the lone calla lily is never alone

elite is recognizing what truly matters
elucidate to others what matters
eloquence is in the Word
elegance is in the simplicity